Happy Halloween!

This book belongs to:

Halloween Costume Parade Coloring Book

Sandy Mahony & Mary Lou Brown

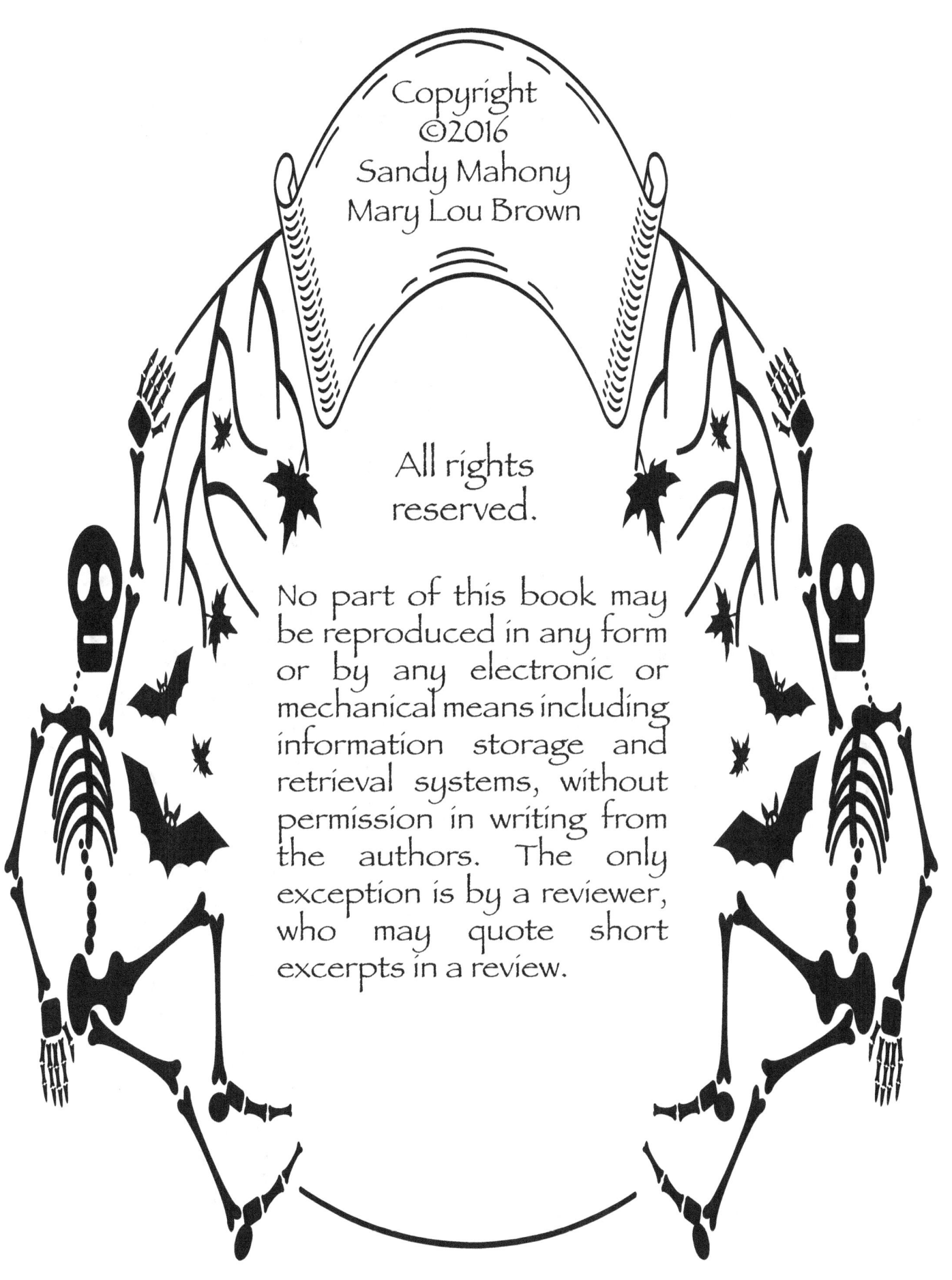

Looking for an idea for a Halloween costume?

Check out the scary costumes we've picked out for you!

Welcome to our Haunted House!

The line starts here for the parade!

happy Halloween

This is not a witch-hunt!

Any luck finding a costume?

adventurelearningpress.com

www.ingramcontent.com/pod-product-compliance
Lightning Source LLC
Chambersburg PA
CBHW081807280526
45789CB00008B/3034